BLOOD, CARNAGE
and the
AGENT PROVOCATEUR

The Constantine Report — Volume One

BLOOD, CARNAGE and the AGENT PROVOCATEUR:

The Truth About The Los Angeles Riots
and the Secret War Against L.A.'s Minorities

by

ALEX CONSTANTINE

THE CONSTANTINE REPORT - Volume One

© 1993

ISBN: 0-938331-04-3

Library of Congress Catalog Card Number: 90-061441

Production and Design: Michael Sheppard

Front cover photo: David Butow / Black Star

Back cover photos: Jeff Share (1 and 3), Peter Turnley (2) / Black Star

Black and white photo credits are listed on page 80

Thanks to Incognito Records, Stuttgart

Printed on acid-free recycled paper

P.O. Box 791
Los Angeles,
CA 90078-0791

Fax: 213-461-8815

CONTENTS

"The teaching of history is that provocation in all countries all times—in France, England, Russia, Germany and in the United States—has been predominately a matter of policy."

—Paul Chevigny
Cops and Rebels, A Study in Provocation

Blood, Carnage and the Agent Provocateur

On the evening of April 29, 1992, the skyline of Los Angeles smoldered in red firelight. The announcement of a verdict in the first Rodney King case was an exhortation to violence, setting off a chain of skirmishes throughout the city—not just at Florence and Normandie. There were, simultaneous with Reginald Denny's torment, reports of looting at Manchester and Vermont, gunfire on Broadway with "numerous people down." At Coliseum Street and Martin Luther King Jr. Boulevard., a group of 20 people pelted rocks at passing cars.[1]

Two weeks later, L.A. Police Chief Daryl F. Gates would tell reporters that the LAPD and FBI were investigating the possibility that the skirmishes were "planned and coordinated" by street gangs. "That's one of the things we are attempting to do," he said, "to see how much of this was planned."[2]

In fact, a task force of 100 investigators from the FBI and other federal, state and local police agencies announced in July 1992 that it had discovered "some organized efforts to attack people and burn stores, but has not found that gangs planned the violence."

Planning and coordination were obvious in the case of Tranh Lam, owner of the Peach Tree Market. At 9:00 p.m., on April 29th, a car full of looters broke into the market. Shortly thereafter, a second car pulled up and disgorged an occupant, who set the store on fire. The next day, Lam's truck was struck from behind. The driver pulled alongside and a passenger opened fire. Lam was hit four times. At that moment, another store owned by Tranh Lam was set aflame.[3]

There were indeed earmarks of planning and coordination on the streets—but not by the volatile street gangs of South-Central Los Angeles.

As smoke and ash began to stain the sky, Vernon Broussard, a national guardsman, and a companion, Jeffrey Sandoval, were driving slowly down Wilshire Boulevard. Both wore dark clothing. The license tags had been downturned so the vehicle couldn't be identified. A passing Beverly Hills cop spotted the tags and stopped the car. Broussard and Sandoval admitted they were armed. Police searched the car and found a .357 magnum. They also turned up two gas cans, glass bottles, rags—the raw ingredients for Molotov cocktails. Suspecting Broussard and Sandoval of participation in the rioting, prosecutors filed felony counts for possession of a flammable substance and possession of incendiary bombs.[4] The prosecution ended in a mistrial when the jury failed to reach a unanimous verdict.[5]

Prosecutors and police were of the opinion that Broussard, the son of a USC professor of education, and his companion meant to take part in the rioting. Deputy District Attorney Carol Nejera argued that they "intended to do something . . . improper and inappropriate." There is disagreement as to whether Broussard was actually called to duty during the riots, as he contended. Defense Attorney Warren Ettinger said that Broussard, who attended the trial in uniform, put in 16-hour shifts on the riot-wracked streets, and returned to duty after a postponement in his arraignment. This is the version reported in the *Los Angeles Times*.[6] That Broussard was assigned to riot duty at all is denied emphatically by Sgt. George Olsen, a public affairs officer for the National Guard. Olsen informed the *Santa Monica Evening Outlook* that Broussard was *never* sent on riot patrol (contradicting his attorney's appeal to sympathy for a battle-scarred soldier). Sgt. Olsen, reported the *Outlook*, "wants to make that very clear."[7]

Broussard told the jury that he ventured into the first tumults of the rioting to help a stranded motorist. The fire bombs discovered in his trunk

Louis Tackwood at the Glass House, former home of the LAPD's Criminal Conspiracy Section

render this defense improbable.

Meanwhile, a former police dog trainer from Hollywood, by his own account, was sent by the LAPD into the anxious heart of Koreatown to discharge flares at Korean-owned shops. His accomplices, equipped with walkie-talkies, timed the firing of the flares with the passing of black motorists to make it appear that they were responsible.

Most people are oblivious to the existence of political provocateurs, but they constitute an important chapter in the history of American rioting, especially since the Vietnam era.

To illustrate: In 1971, Lee Smith, an ex-convict from the California Men's Colony, testified before Congress that he'd been paid to foment prison unrest. He'd been instructed by authorities to blame "Marxist revolutionary forces" for stirring up the violence. Afterward, conditions at the penal colony worsened.[8]

Louis Tackwood, formerly an undercover operative of the LAPD's Criminal Conspiracy Section (CCS), defined an agent provocateur as "a police agent who is introduced to any political organization with instructions to foment discontent."[9] A provocateur incites violence, giving authorities a justification to respond.

A quarter century of provocateur-inspired civil disturbances reflect on the turmoil of May 1992. Tackwood, who'd been recruited by CCS to provoke prison riots, blew the whistle in 1971, charging that the secret LAPD unit had been "set up on the same basis as the CIA."[10] CCS agents, he told the press, "went to Washington, D.C., and at one time or another have been trained by the Federal Bureau." Tackwood disclosed that the agents of CCS were sponsored by the federal intelligence apparatus: "Like J. Edgar Hoover said, 'They're my boys, they're my boys.'"

Mike Rothmiller

The Tackwood revelations converged with the Watergate scandal and the White House Plumbers unit, which is alleged to have spent $10 million on political provocations and other forms of subterfuge.[11] The CCS was directly linked to the Washington, D.C.-based Inter-Agency Group on Domestic Intelligence and Internal Security, a little-known covert operations unit made up of right-wing agents from the FBI, CIA, the Defense Intelligence Agency (DIA), National Security Council, Army, Air Force, Navy and local police departments.[12]

Federal intelligence agencies still mesh with the LAPD, especially the Organized Crime Intelligence Division (OCID). Mike Rothmiller, a former OCID detective, stumbled upon the symbiosis and summarily fell prey to an assailant's bullet. The chief suspect in the attempted murder, Jack Ingraham, is a wealthy Orange County employee of an aircraft leasing firm at John Wayne Airport. Ingraham is also reputed to have smuggled arms into Latin America and cocaine back to the U.S.

Rothmiller had been investigating another suspected cocaine courier, Marina del Rey resident Robert Terry, when the assailant stopped him. Terry, once a NYPD officer, is a frequent traveler to Washington, D.C. "He has big connections," says Rothmiller, "including the CIA." Terry once donated $25,000 to the GOP for a set of White House china and posed for a photograph with Nancy Reagan. Detective Rothmiller's prime informant in the Terry investigation was Herman Ferriola, a repatriated ex-general of the Mexicas Federales. Ferriola has often been seen tooling around L.A. in a squad car loaned him by the chief of the North Las Vegas Police Department. He has, says Rothmiller, "the deepest access to the Mexican intelligence community. U.S. agents, spies and cops buzzed around him like gringo bees." Ferriola is close to a host of LAPD officers,

was once a major in the Colombian secret police and has served under Arturo Durazo, the corrupt former Mexican police chief.

Based on Ferriola's information, Rothmiller tipped the IRS, who followed Robert Terry's movements on a sojourn to Washington, D.C. They tailed the drug courier from the airport to the Executive Office Building of the White House.

Since the shooting of Rothmiller by a suspected drug smuggler working on behalf of the CIA, the disabled detective has been frozen out, denied a pension, denied benefits by the police department.[13]

At the 1990 trial of LASD Deputy Daniel Garner and former Sheriff's Sgt. Robert Sobel, accused of skimming drugs and profits from an "elite" LASD task force, a gag order was imposed against any mention of CIA complicity. They and other officers testified that the unit cooperated with the CIA in the laundering of drug proceeds. The funds were sent back to Latin American drug cartels. The sheriffs were told that the money trail was followed to gather information on the cartels. Harland Braun, representing Deputy Garner, acknowledged in the courtroom that "numerous documents indicating that drug money was being used to purchase military equipment for Central America" had been turned up by the accused officers. U.S. District Judge Edward Rafeedie ruled the testimony "irrelevant" and forbade further discussion of CIA money laundering in his courtroom.[14]

It's not as if the city hadn't been warned that the LAPD was more deeply involved in right-wing political malfeasance than any other metropolitan police force. Tackwood pulled LAPD skeletons out of the closet with the publication of *The Glass House Tapes* in 1973, including the disclosure that the department had about about 125 provocateurs on

Michael Zinzin

the payroll. Some in the press, not many, asked questions. Liberal community groups in Los Angeles, discovering they'd been infiltrated, sued the LAPD. CCS, the secret police unit, was disbanded, its spies and provocateurs reassigned. In its place evolved the OCID, which incidentally maintains no files on organized crime. The OCID does, however, keep extensive files on local politicians and private citizens.[15] Another offshoot is the LAPD's Anti-Terrorist Division, headed until recently by the former chief's brother, Stephen Gates. A staffer, asking not to be identified, charged that the unit maintains files on City Council members. In 1988, Robert Vernon, an assistant police chief assigned to the division, forked over $3.8-million worth of penance in a lawsuit filed by Michael Zinzin, a Pasadena City Council member, who resented that secret police files were kept by Vernon in an attempt to discredit him.[16]

In a local speech, Zinzin linked the LAPD intelligence cadres to ultra-right-wing organizations. Information gathered by the LAPD, he discovered, was turned over to the John Birch Society and recited into the Congressional Record by the late Congressman Larry MacDonald, who perished in the downing of KAL Flight 007. The information flow, said Zinzin, resulted in the murders of activists, political bombings and the planting of false information in the press. The intelligence faction of the LAPD, he found, was linked to the political network that "was also involved in the attempt to overthrow the Nicaraguan government," and "conjured up the war in the Middle East." Zinzin's report on the LAPD, sponsored by the Coalition Against Police Abuse, describes rampant abuse of authority. In 1989-90 there were 3,179 investigations of the department by Internal Affairs of "violations of policy, lying, theft and all kinds of corruption" by 3,590 officers. All told, *one-third* of the LAPD

(Original AP captions) Top: MOVING IN—Members of the LAPD motorcycle unit move onto the taxiway at L.A. International Airport after an explosive device was discovered and later detonated. Bottom: PROUD AND SAD—Senior L.A. police officers stand at a police headquarters press conference during a major announcement by Chief Daryl Gates regarding the airport bomb scare. Police are happy the suspect was uncovered quickly, but sad it was one of their own. Inset: Jimmy Wade Pearson

force was under investigation. "If that's not a police department out of control, I don't know what is," Zinzin said.

The Police Commission banned the practice of spying on political figures in 1984.

Nonetheless, Attorney Geoffrey Taylor Gibbs of the John M. Langston Bar Association testified before the Christopher Commission on May 1, 1992 that "the belief is widespread in this city that Chief Gates, much like J. Edgar Hoover, maintains files of personal and political information on every major political figure in Los Angeles."[17] Three weeks later, Mary Henry of the Compton school board assailed the L.A. City Council: "You have city councilmen involved in *drugs*," she said, "and the police know about it and choose to keep the lid on those people by threatening them."[18]

Indications that spies and provocateurs continued to be employed by the LAPD surfaced in 1984 with the arrest of Jimmy Wade Pearson, an officer of the Metro Division assigned to the Olympic games. At first, Pearson was publicly lauded for disarming a pipe-bomb planted in a wheel well of a bus filled with the baggage of 52 Turkish athletes, who occupied another bus parked nearby.

Chief Gates praised the 40-year-old officer for a "helluva courageous act." The discovery of the bomb necessitated the evacuation of hundreds from Terminal Two at the L.A. Airport. Two "terrorist" groups claimed responsibility for the bomb, the Justice Commandos of Armenian Genocide and the Armenian Secret Army. The *Los Angeles Times* ran a lengthy history of strained Turkish-Armenian relations from 1915 onward.[19]

Alas, the following day a wilted Daryl Gates announced that Pearson had been arrested for constructing and planting the bomb himself. Pearson

Top: Donald Segretti—Bottom: William Lemmer

was held at Parker Center with bail set at $60,000. At a press conference, Gates took credit for solving the case. He explained that Pearson, a former Navy SEAL, only intended to impress his superiors at the Metro Division. "He wanted to do something that would cause them to take notice," Gates said, "and certainly we have noticed him."[20] In October 1985, L.A. Superior Court Judge Gerald Levie waived sentencing. He ordered Pearson to perform 1,500 hours of community service—very lenient considering that pipe-bombs are "notoriously unstable," according to Arleigh McGree, head of the LAPD bomb squad, because gun powder embedded in the pipe threads can ignite an explosion.[21]

"The basic thing is he did not attempt to hurt anybody," Judge Levie noted.

The LAPD intelligence unit—despite public denial—was established wholly for purposes of political sabotage. Before the arrests at Watergate and the possibility of public exposure of White House involvement, CCS was cut into a plan to incite a riot at the Miami Republican convention in 1972. Hundreds of Republicans were recruited by Nixon aide Donald Segretti of Watergate fame, and Douglas Caddy, head of Young Americans for Freedom.[22] Planning and coordination were handled by Edward Birch of the FBI and Sgt. Daniel Mahoney of the CCS. Tackwood's disclosures were confirmed by former Green Beret and FBI provocateur William Lemmer, who testified before a Florida grand jury that he'd been instrumental in a homicidal strategy to disrupt the 1972 Republican convention by organizing "fire teams" armed with automatic weapons and incendiary devices. He said paid provocateurs intended to "fire lead weights, 'fried' marbles, ball bearings, cherry bombs, smoke bombs by means of wrist rockets, sling shots and crossbows."[23]

The torched ROTC building at Kent State University

Two years before, witnesses of the rioting at Kent State University testified that provocateurs were responsible for the pandemonium there. The grand jury investigation of the demonstration concluded that many of the rioters "were not students, but were of a type who always welcome the opportunity to participate in the destruction of property."[24] The National Guard only cracked down on the students when the dilapidated ROTC building, with its full ammunition stores, was torched and went up like a Rapture. "One very interesting thing that came out of that," one Kent State student recalled: "The ROTC building is about 200 feet from the police station, right across the courtyard. All these self-styled revolutionaries who were burning down the ROTC building *took 45 minutes to get it started. All the time, the police never attempted to stop them.* In fact, it was almost as if they *wanted* them to burn down the ROTC building. From this point on, they used this as an *excuse* to stop the movement that students were involved in—the massive opposition to the war in Vietnam."[25]

Police and military units were held back, the rioting escalated—just as police docility at Florence and Normandie Avenues on April 29, 1992 permitted pandemonium to explode from a small pocket of outrage.

From the *Los Angeles Times*:

The police department has come under fire for pulling back from the South Los Angeles intersection of Florence and Normandie Avenues, where some of the earliest violence was reported, and for failing to redeploy for hours. It was during this period that unsuspecting and defenseless motorists were dragged from their cars and brutally beaten in horrifying scenes broadcast live on television.[26]

A provocateur is an infiltrator, a Judas who espouses and begets violence, setting others up for arrest and prosecution. Secret police

(AP caption) The Reverend Jesse Jackson tries to console UCLA student Monique Mathews as the Crenshaw Medical Square burns in the background

operations like the LAPD's are quietly tied to the DIA, which has operated on a budget ten times that of the FBI and CIA combined. Provocateur actions, linked with CIA- and DIA-backed police units and SWAT teams, are explosive. Spawned by the CIA and Army in 1968, SWAT troopers trained in riot control at a camp secreted inside Fort Gordon, Georgia.

Inevitably the investigation following a provocateur action is conducted by defense intelligence officials (the Webster Commission, a prime example, allowed the LAPD to read and criticize its report prior to release), followed by increases in funding for undercover law enforcement, more spying on civilians, secret files, harsher police tactics.[27] This is the aftermath of the riots in Los Angeles.

Residents of South-Central Los Angeles said that they'd witnessed arsonists who were clearly not locals. They were seen lighting fires and escaped before residents could stop them.[28] After touring riot-torn sections of Los Angeles, the Rev. Jesse Jackson held a televised press conference. He said a burned-out hospital he'd visited appeared to him to be a professional arson job. On the subject of fires, Charlie Parsons of the FBI said that his task force had uncovered evidence of business owners engaging in "arson for profit."[29]

A delay by police at the onset of a riot invites the escalation of bloodshed. Police inaction is another form of provocation. There are precursors: The 1970 State Prison riot in New Mexico was pitched into mass torture and murder when police and prison guards were ordered not to intervene. Events leading up to the riot suggest that it was encouraged by prison officials. Three weeks before rioting broke out, Raymond Procunier, San Francisco's Undersheriff (the brains behind the brains of provocations at San Quentin, the murder of George Jackson and the

Cell block six at the New Mexico State Penitentiary on February 4, 1980

prosecution of the Soledad brothers) arrived in New Mexico to "consult" with officials of the correctional facility. Soon thereafter, prison bars separating the main office from the control center were replaced with "unbreakable" glass. The prison atmosphere was agitated by informants, universally despised by prisoners.

When rioting broke out, a Niagara of "unbreakable" glass showered the concourse and corridor. Outside, police and prison guards passively observed the rioting through binoculars while hostages were tortured, mutilated, blinded with soldering irons, shot and decapitated. When it was over, every prisoner in the witness protection program, sequestered in a separate high-security compound, was dead. As at Kent State and Los Angeles, responsible officials refused to call in the police until violence was rampant.[30]

L.A. Police Chief Daryl Gates—a veteran of CCS and the OCID—blamed public criticism of the department for police inaction. Gates suggested that members of the Webster Commission "take a look at some of the mental [attitudes] that have been building in this Department for over a year of constant criticism," and how morale may have affected the response. He accused the press of engaging in a "feeding frenzy", of "*beating up* on my police officers."[31]

Chief Gates has also laid blame on Lt. Mike Moulin for faults in response to the rioting. "Moulin," reported the *Times*, "who has been *ordered not to comment*, pulled a group of officers back from a melee at Florence and Normandie about 5:45 p.m., April 29, an hour before motorists and truck driver Reginald O. Denny were yanked from their vehicles and attacked by a stone-throwing mob."[32]

Lt. Moulin answered the recrimination with a $30-million slander suit

Top: Mike Moulin—Bottom: Daryl Gates

against Chief Gates in October, and filed a claim for damages against the city. Moulin argued that he was only a scapegoat, that it was not within his authority to order officers to Florence and Normandie. "While Chief Gates was attending the fund-raiser in Brentwood," Moulin said in his lawsuit, "those of us in uniform were left to handle a highly volatile situation." When assigning blame, he said, "perhaps the chief should look in the mirror." At a press conference the same afternoon, Gates dismissed Moulin's slander suit as a disguised effort to land "a disability pension." Gates sniffed, "That might be what he is trying to do."[33]

In May, Gates had argued in his own defense that a family emergency had preoccupied him during the riots. On a book tour to publicize his autobiography, *Chief: My Life in the LAPD*, he claimed that his son's drug overdose "was deeply on my mind during the riot." Speaking of his son Scott, the LAPD's highest official lamented, "They thought he was going to die." Gates had to admit, though, that he failed to visit his hospitalized son, nor had he seen him since his release and recovery from the overdose. But he denied that the story was a play for sympathy. The overdose, Gates said on the Phil Donahue show, "was extremely distracting to me. It's always on your mind. It's a constant ache on the middle of your chest."[34]

Police disarray at the initial phase of the rioting in L.A. was aggravated by the absence of hundreds of LAPD captains, who were attending a training seminar in Oxnard. Chief Gates left Parker Center as the riot began to take in a fund-raiser against Proposition F, a ballot measure that would make the police chief more accountable to the city. He had announced a $1-million increase in overtime revenue, yet officers by the hundreds were allowed to go home at the end of the afternoon shift.

Chief Gates offered as partial explanation for the delay that police were

busy protecting firefighters, but the *Times* reported that "angry city fire officials" disputed his contention. "Fire officials said that in fact they got only limited protection during the first hours of the riot, even though large numbers of officers were kept waiting at a command post at 54th and Arlington Streets."

Police commissioners were deluged with complaints. Where were the police? Some 200 officers, ordered to do nothing, were appalled. They stood around waiting for orders while the carnage escalated. The paralysis of police response continued into the second day. One deputy chief harshly criticized the department as the riot gathered momentum: "This is alien to everything we're supposed to do in a situation like this."[35]

From the *New York Times*:

LOS ANGELES, May 6—Emerging evidence from the first crucial hours after the acquittal of four police officers in the beating of Rodney G. King provides the strong indication that top police officials did little to plan for the possibility of violence and did not follow standard procedures to contain rioting once it began.

An examination of television news tapes and police radio transmissions, as well as interviews with city officials, shows that the police never put into effect their standard riot-control strategy. . . . The police retreated as the violence began, but violated the *basic police procedure* for riot-control by failing to cordon off the area around one of the first trouble spots and not returning to that area for hours.

Police 911 dispatchers attempted to send squad cars to the scene of the first violent outbreaks, but were repeatedly ignored or overruled.[36]

A thick scallop of smoke hovered over L.A. Fires had been set from Hollywood to the southern tip of the city. Outbursts of rioting were reported in Long Beach, the harbor area, the San Fernando Valley and Panorama City.

Two days later, the city now in turmoil, Gov. Wilson and Mayor

Gen. William Harrison

Bradley phoned the White House. At 7:15 a.m., it was announced that 200 officers from the U.S. Marshall's paramilitary "Special Operations Group" (veterans of the 1990 Panama invasion) and a Desert Storm battalion would be mustered in L.A. to "ensure the safety of the streets."[37]

National Guard forces were long overdue. They were greeted by the rage of city residents who had lost homes and businesses to fire. Between the initial call for Guard units and the arrival of the riot-control equipment, 17 hours passed. It was not until the morning of April 30th that a Guard helicopter loaded ammunition, equipment and body armor at Camp Roberts, the Paso Robles training base. Guard officials claimed that the helicopter had been unable to load at night because there were "no lights" (!) at the Camp Roberts airstrip.

The explanation for the delay given by retired Sixth Army Gen. William Harrison is a masterful interweaving of alibis and tragic decisions. Harrison reviewed the Guard's performance from the initial dispatch, and discovered that Sacramento first ordered up a C-130 cargo plane to move ammunition and hardware, decided against it, called in a single CH-47 helicopter instead—*four hours* after the mobilization order was given. This was at 1:20 a.m., April 30th. The chopper was delayed at Stockton when the flight crew realized gas masks might be needed. A supply of masks was hauled aboard.

The helicopter decamped, settled down at Camp Roberts in San Luis Obispo County. The CH-47 refueled, Harrison explained, far from the munitions dump. A truck was therefore needed to shuttle supplies *to* the helicopter. Alas, it was discovered that obsolete *hand grenades* (?) had been put aboard. These were unloaded and replaced. The military hardware was finally sent on its way at 9:45 a.m., but the helicopter was rerouted to

CONCHITA
RESTAURANTE Y PUPUSERIA
384-4177

pick up more ammunition at a nearby military base—a "cost-cutting" measure, Gen. Harrison reported with a face as straight as a mausoleum slab—to avoid squandering the use of another copter. Somehow two-and-a-half hours slipped by. When it landed, the chopper was already packed to the gunwales. Even Gen. Harrison couldn't account for the lapse of time. It finally lifted off from from San Luis Obispo at 12:20 in the afternoon, bound for Los Angeles, arriving at 3:35 p.m.[38]

In the meantime, some 23,000 calls were made to 911 emergency operators. But Guard units were deployed at a trickle by Daryl Gates, who took command of police and Guard mobilization efforts himself, calling it an "experiment in community-based policing."[39]

Gates immediately proceeded to sabotage any effort to quell the riot.

Others around him tried desperately to explain why Gates kept hamstringing troop mobilization. Stanley Sheinbaum, president of the Police Commission, opined sympathetically that the Chief's "pride" slowed deployment. Jesse Brewer, another commissioner, offered that Gates was "reluctant" to use the Guard because "the Chief likes to feel he can handle everything by himself, without any help from anybody." Deputy Mayor Mark Fabiani was equally solicitous in defense of his police chief: "There is always resistance on the part of local authorities to call on outside sources."[40] "Where Guardsmen were in place," reported the *Times* on May 6, "their ranks were sometimes stretched perilously thin."

At Florence and Normandie, rancor arising from the Rodney King decision caught fire. Residents of the area swept into the streets shouting with a Biblical vengeance.

"If the police hadn't started harassing us, we'd have all walked back to the house and the riot would never have started," said Mark Jackson, the

Reginald and Ashley Denny

half-brother of Damian Monroe Williams. Jackson wasn't the only one of that opinion: Compton City Councilwoman Patricia Moore caused a furor among LAPD loyalists when she publicly stated at a funeral for two officers slain in an unrelated incident that the police and government started the riot. Georgiana Williams, Damian's mother, told reporters for National Public Radio on April 13th, 1993 that the violence occurred after a sequence of events beginning with the King verdict. Mark Jackson, her son, and a friend, Kermit, spotted a 16-year-old neighbor hopping a fence to evade police. Mark yelled at the officers. The police threw the young man "back across the fence, and they were beating him," she said, "and everyone was screaming, 'Leave him alone, leave him alone!' Then the officers took Mark and mashed his head into the car. This is when everyone got angry and took it to the streets. If the police had not beat Mark and Kermit in front of the community, nothing would have happened." To be sure, videotapes of the initial conflict show police harassment of the congregation, kicking off the riot.

When the Florence and Normandie crowd swelled to 150, jamming and jostling the police skirmish line, the LAPD retreated. "With the police gone," Peter Boyer wrote in the *New Yorker*, "there was suddenly a power vacuum in South Central."[41] The moiling crowd was in a black mood. Someone shouted directions, "Leave the Mexicans alone, we're only getting the Buddha-heads and white boys."[42]

Truck driver Reginald Denny drove into the melee with his radio tuned to a music station, unaware that a verdict in the King case had been announced. The madness on the street was an alarming anomaly to him. Something shattered his windshield. Denny doesn't remember anything else of the assault that left him broken and bleeding on the street.

Some gang members called the riot a "slave rebellion," and African-Americans are widely regarded as the sole instigators. However, of some 5,000 people first arrested for looting, assault and destruction of property, 52 percent were Latino.[43] Perhaps to cover their own part in fomenting violence, a "special police intelligence" unit circulated a memo on May 8, 1992 to station patrol units falsely claiming that the bloodshed had been instigated by "Crips and Bloods from the housing projects . . . united under the direction and leadership of Muslims." The L.A. Coalition Against Police Abuse has called this memo blatant disinformation, reminiscent of the FBI's COINTELPRO, yet Chief Gates would later echo this fabrication in the press. "All of the housing project gangs have united," the memo claimed, adding that the purpose of gang rallies attended by hundreds of youths "has been to develop strategy and tactics for killing cops." Furthermore, the so-called intelligence report stated that gang members wanted to make a statement "by overtaking and seizing a police station," and starting a "war."[44] The hyperbolic rhetoric of fictional, gang-baiting "intelligence" reports like the May 8th memo gave rise to a task force of 100 FBI and assorted federal agents, coordinated with L.A. cops, looking for the "ringleaders" of the riot. The D.A. and U.S Attorney's offices went so far as to return RICO-organized criminal conspiracy charges against gang leaders.[45]

The *genuine* conspiracy lurks in the "Street Terrorism Enforcement and Prevention Act", or STEP, legislating the implementation of a blacklisting database of gang members for local law enforcement. Having one's name in the database is prosecutable as a felony offense apart from any other criminal charges.[46]

Crips and Bloods were scapegoated by police and FBI with

Left to right: Antoine Miller, Henry Watson and Damian Williams

McCarthyesque vigor. The *Los Angeles Times* chased shadows when it reported that the suspects in the Denny riot-beating case were "said to be members of, or affiliated with, the 8-Trey Gangster Crips, one of Los Angeles' most notorious street gangs." Charlie Parsons, special agent in charge of the local FBI bureau, snaffled a toothly grimace at reporters: "I don't think these communities will be upset to see gang members arrested," he said, alluding to the L.A. 4. Mumbled retractions soon followed when Officer Michael McMahon, the source of the accusation, turned out to be the subject of an administrative probe. The court transcript was shed of his testimony.[47]

Every one of the L.A. 4 has a criminal record. Damian Williams and Antoine Miller have long juvenile arrest histories.[48] Williams was twice charged with auto theft, but has never been convicted. The charges were dropped. Why? Henry Keith Watson is accused of holding Denny down while others beat him and smashed his head with a brick. Watson once looted an armored car of $6,620.10, pled guilty, but was sentenced to a mere 90-day jail term and probation by Superior Court Judge Gordon Ringer. [49]

The L.A. riot was punctuated by the King- and Denny-beating trials. The Simi Valley trial of LAPD officers Koon *et al* was a degrading performance. Nine of the jurors were white, eight had served in the military. Two of the jurors were U.S. Marines. One was an ex-security officer with a history of using excessive force. (*Another* security guard with a violent past somehow turned up on the jury for the second trial.) During court breaks, the jury openly expressed admiration for police.[50]

Equally corrupt, the Reginald Denny case threatened to veer off the docket in October 1992 when L.A. Superior Court Judge John Ouderkirk

Fredrick Celani on October 3, 1984

ordered an inquiry into whether an attorney for Williams took directions from a CIA/FBI operative attempting to sabotage the defense.[51]

Accused of behind-the-scenes interference was the now-defunct Center for Constitutional Law and Justice, a nonprofit law firm in North Hollywood.[52] Former directors contended that the legal center was in reality a covert intelligence unit posing as a liberal counterpoint to the LA district attorney's office.[53] In a May 1992 speech in Pasadena before Individuals Making a Difference, Fredrick "Sebastian" Celani, the firm's deputy director, claimed that the center handled a case load of 1,300 clients. Of those, 1,100 were inmates of the federal and state prison system, mostly drug offenders.

In August, the Center withdrew from the Denny case and fired Williams' defense attorney Dennis Palmieri, who claims to be Jesus Christ and that George Bush has conspired with Margaret Thatcher to steal his private thoughts. "There are people who have told me I'm Satan," says Palmieri.[54] However eccentric, he was ruled a competent attorney by Judge Ouderkirk.

The deputy director of the Center for Constitutional Law and Justice, Fredrick George Celani, also known as Fred Sebastian, was known to Los Angeles radio listeners as the boisterous talk show host of "Civil Liberties" on KIEV-AM. And he is a CIA operative, according to a sworn 1991 California Central District Court affidavit filed by Celani. His employment with the CIA, he writes in the affidavit, has involved him in investment fraud, drug smuggling, domestic intelligence and infiltration of the Hollywood entertainment industry. [55]

The use of legal organizations for intelligence purposes is not unprecedented. The International Commission of Jurists, for example, a worldwide attorney association, was for ten years partly financed (and used) by the CIA, according to former agent Philip Agee.[56] Since the mid-'80s from Terminal Island Prison, Celani directed a public-interest legal firm that represented drug dealers, "subversives" and racketeers. "He actually had some success in this line . . . by utilizing his *remarkable access to prison offices*," Boyer writes. The affidavit details Celani's background in the CIA, filed nearly two years before his involvement in the Williams case. It fully supports his contention that the Justice Department, the CIA and FBI are involved in sabotaging criminal defense cases. In separate interviews, attorneys employed by Celani echoed the sabotage allegation.

Celani writes in his Central District Court affidavit that his superiors gave him names to target for information-gathering. All legal work, according to Celani, was handled by Justice Department attorneys. The firm's legal summaries were modeled after FBI field reports. In less than three years, over 5,000 reports were filed by Celani's legal firm. Prospective clients were solicited with a letter tailored to a defendant's specific legal and financial needs.

Prison guards, he says, upon learning that Celani was a CIA agent, revealed to him that the brother of Wisconsin Gov. Tom Thompson ran a major drug distribution ring, an enterprise widely reported in Milwaukee newspapers and the *Wisconsin State Journal*, but ultimately denied by the state court.

Celani says he assumed the post of manager for the Young People's campaign and gathered intelligence on the Democratic Party and Gov. Jerry Brown. Also in the early '80s he was steeped in money laundering and cocaine importation. He sojourned to Springfield, Illinois and started an overnight air courier operation called Kayport to move narcotics and launder the proceeds.

According to Boyer, "The town fathers embraced Celani and his partner. The two men took in more that two hundred thousand dollars of investors' money, opened Kayport Package Express, and shut it down six days later. Celani was indicted on 15 racketeering and fraud charges, convicted on all counts in 1985."[57]

During his pre-prison tenure in Los Angeles, he says, the CIA developed an international network of investment fronts, banks and computer systems, "one of the most sophisticated and fruitful federal government intelligence-gathering operations ever attempted in the United States." The hub of the computer operation was a high-security compound located at 16161 Ventura Boulevard in Encino, and later moved to the Galleria Towers complex in Sherman Oaks.

Another computer system, used to store information on private citizens, was maintained at a CIA front in Cheektowaga, New York, just south of Buffalo. "The building sat opposite the Buffalo International Airport," Celani wrote in the affidavit, "which allowed us access to underground conduits that ran to a Westinghouse facility located on airport property [with] direct lines to Washington, D.C." Here, data concerning the political beliefs of thousands of students, their social, sexual and intellectual philosophies were collected.

In 1985, Celani wrote a book about his work entitled, *The Best Politicians Money Can Buy*, later retitled *D.R.E.A.M.S.* (*Los Angeles Times* reporter Jim Newton, interviewed for this story, has obtained a copy.) Because the manuscript deals with the CIA, it was sent to Langley for review by Agency officials. Its inflammatory content—and political

Dennis Palmieri

pressure from Wisconsin Gov. Thompson—led to a conviction for racketeering on July 19, 1985. Celani received a 15-year sentence, cut short after submitting his CIA background in the affidavit for habeas corpus. While sequestered in prison, he was tapped by the FBI to gather intelligence on Mafia capos and narcotics traffickers. Celani claims he continued to be held in custody despite a Congressionally-sanctioned grant of immunity and reward for cooperation.

From Terminal Island, Celani launched the Center for Constitutional Law and Justice. "He brought in a lot of dough," one attorney employed at the firm told Boyer. "If anyone was to guess, it was probably somewhere around four million bucks."[58] A year after his parole, he ordered Center attorney Dennis Palmieri to offer free legal services to Damian Monroe Williams, one of the accused tormentors of Reginald Denny.[59] Palmieri located the mother of Damian Williams and took him on as a client. But in August of 1992, Palmieri testified, "I was ordered by Mr. Celani not to spend any more time on the case." Celani told Palmieri that Williams "could spend the rest of his life in jail for all he cared, that Mr. Williams was guilty, that he did not care if Damian died or got his head chopped off." Celani forced him to withdraw a motion to suppress a confession by Williams, whom Celani referred to as "scum," and "a criminal."[60]

Yvonne Brathwaite Burke, the recently elected county supervisor, opined that Williams might have reason to demand a new preliminary hearing. [61] "Celani turned out to be an ex-convict," the *Los Angeles Times* reported, "with a history of defrauding people." One FBI agent called Celani "the most complete sociopath I've ever seen in my life."[62] From Los Angeles he moved to Little Rock, Arkansas, and was summarily arrested for wire fraud and bribery of a federal judge.

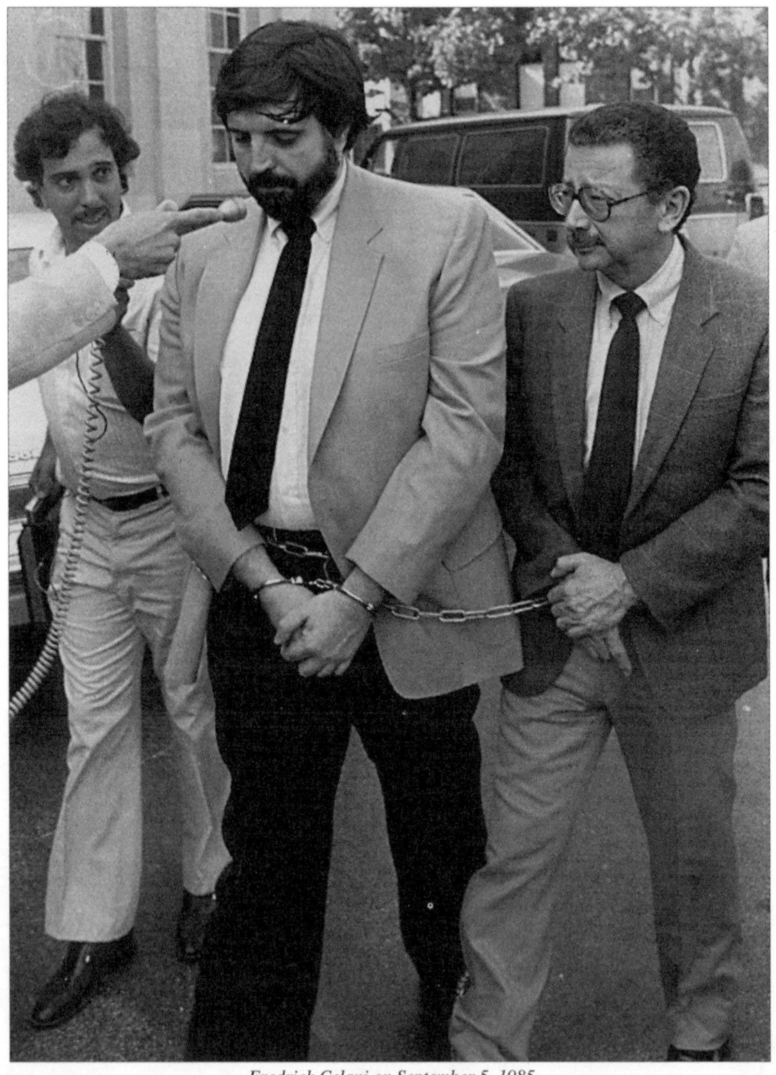

Fredrick Celani on September 5, 1985

Fred Celani claims that "the riots were fomented by federal agents."

His credibility is considered nil, but equally so is the credibility of public news sources of greater L.A. The *Los Angeles Times*, like Judge Ouderkirk, neglected to discuss Celani's contention that the Center was in fact an FBI cover directed by a CIA con man. The *Times* has made much of the fact that Celani is a liar, but CIA operators are liars by definition. The *Times* itself has not been altogether honest as regards the enigmatic Fred Celani. Any mention of his 1991 court affidavit—sworn, signed and filed under penalty of perjury—has been suppressed, and therefore so has his self-described background as a CIA plunderer and pariah. A *Times* critique falsely accused Celani of stating that right-wing radio and television personality Rush Limbaugh and Rep. Robert Dornan (R-Garden Grove) are engaged in a homosexual relationship. He never said this. Celani only maintained that he'd been assigned to *follow* these Republican extremists. The *Times*, in other words, smeared Celani with a flat-out libel.[63]

Like the defense team in the Denny riot-beating trial, the "blue-ribbon" commission assembled to investigate causes of the riot was an insidious lot. The Christopher panel was well-represented by the military and industrial sector of California politics. Leading lights on the commission included:

• Warren Christopher—attorney for IBM and Lockheed Corp., which is closely aligned with the CIA, board member of the all-white California Club until his recent State Dept. appointment, vice chair of the McCone Commission, which investigated the Watts riots, headed by former CIA Director John McCone. In January 1993, before the Senate Foreign Relations Committee, Secretary of State-designate Christoper testified

Secretary of State Warren Christopher

regarding his knowledge of military intelligence gathering on U.S. civilians during the 1960s, contradicting prior testimony given at a 1977 confirmation hearing.

• John Arguelles—active in Republican political politics, retired California Supreme Court justice, appointed at the request of Police Chief Gates.

• Roy Anderson—chairman emeritus of Lockheed Corp., on the board of directors of Interstate Bank Corp. and Southern California Edison.

• Willie Barnes—one of only two blacks on the panel, a former California Commissioner of Corporations.

• Richard Mosk—member of the Iran-U.S. Claims Tribunal, staffer for the Warren Commission, which suppressed the truth of the John Kennedy assassination.

• Mickey Kantor—a Los Angeles lawyer and well-known Democratic party strategist.

• Andrea Sheridan Ordin—recently resigned her position as a California assistant attorney general.

The roots of the Christopher and Webster Commissions are embedded in the same Washington-based power control group behind a host of political assassinations, drug scandals, cover-ups and sundry other political horror stories. Mickey Kantor, Bill Clinton's choice for U.S. Trade Representative, and Willie Barnes, for instance, have both worked closely with Washington attorney Charles Mannatt, former Democratic party chairman.[64] Mannatt was instrumental in the establishment of a capitalization fund for the Credit International Bank in Washington, D.C.,[65] along with Director of Central Intelligence Richard Allen and Edwin Fullner of the right-wing Heritage Foundation. The bank was a CIA

Top: Clarence Kelley—Bottom: Hubert Williams

creation and channel for drug money filtered through Swiss accounts.[66]

The Christopher and Webster Commissions both drew on the resources of the Police Foundation in Washington, D.C., which receives half of its funding from the Justice Dept.'s Law Enforcement Assistance Administration (LEAA).[67] Hubert Williams, a former Newark police chief, is president of the tax-supported "think tank," which is ultra-right in political orientation but parades in public as a liberal organization. Clarence Kelley, former director of the FBI, is treasurer. Kelley is well known for his contributions to the keeping of secret computer files on private citizens, FBI harassment of blacks and "subversives," and civil repression following disturbances incited by FBI provocateurs. The late Robert Kasanov, attorney and Police Foundation director, has represented Michele Sindona (the financial liaison between the Vatican, Mafia and the P-2 Freemasonic Lodge in the laundering of drug profits).[68] Kasanov also performed legal work for Wedtech's Robert Wallach, and Andrew Crispo, who continues to be a suspect in the New York "death mask" torture-murder of Eigil Vesti, a gay fashion model.[69] (Crispo was acquitted in a rigged jury trial, a corruption of the judicial process of which Kasanov had full knowledge.[70]) The *Washington Post* ran an exposé in June 1991 linking Police Foundation officer Thomas Pownell to Melvin R. Paisley, the scandal-ridden former CEO of the Martin Marietta Corp., a primary defense contractor.[71] Foundation officer Fred Hartley was the chairman of Unocal Oil Corp. Some think tank.

In a profile on Hubert Williams, the *Los Angeles Times* somehow missed the criminal and ultra-conservative connections, and lauded the Foundation's "reputation for spawning innovative, progressive policing."[72] Williams sits on the advisory board of the Rand Corp.'s Drug

Dr. Louis West

Policy Research Center. He also participated, with Chief Gates, in the executive session on policing at Harvard's John F. Kennedy School of Government, the leading CIA-influenced academic institution. In recent years, during Williams' tenure at the helm of the Police Foundation, the quality and significance of the research has declined.

The Foundation is a conduit of LEAA funding. The LEAA has also lent generous support to such ominous projects as UCLA's proposed Center for the Study of the Causes and Reduction of Violence—a regimen of surgical brain experimentation on African-American and Latino prisoners, supposedly to isolate and control cerebral causes of crime.[73] The project was based on the work of UCLA's Drs. Vernon Mark and Frank Ervin, "pioneers" of brain alteration at Boston City Hospital, who claimed that one operation they'd performed was "a great success" though the subject later committed suicide.[74] The UCLA proposal was submitted to the California Criminal Justice Dept. by Dr. Louis West, a former CIA mind control specialist, currently director of UCLA's Neuropsychiatric Institute.[75] The proposal was killed when the Federation of American Scientists complained publicly that the psychosurgical center was a throwback to Nazi Germany.

Other LEAA programs, in violation of the Nuremburg and AMA codes, have included the testing of Prolixin on 1,093 subjects at Vacaville Prison and the involuntary sterilization of hundreds of prisoners, rationalized as a "preventative procreation" measure by the courts.[76]

William Webster was plucked from the same secret governmental circles as Christopher *et al*. The presiding investigator of the Webster Commission is a veteran of COINTELPRO, the FBI's secret war against the Black Panthers—28 were murdered—and other radical

William Webster and Hubert Williams

organizations.[77] In March 1991, Sen. John Kerry's (D-Mass.) investigation of CIA complicity in the operation of the Bank of Credit and Commerce International (BCCI) was ignored and stonewalled by William Webster. Kerry wrote Webster, requesting a report on the bank's criminal activities, including loans made to Iraq preceding the Kuwaiti conflict. "For two months no reply came," writes David Corn, a columnist for *The Nation*. "In the meantime, BCCI was shut down. While waiting for Webster, the subcommittee received a briefing from the CIA on its knowledge of the bank, focusing mostly on BCCI money laundering, by then a matter of public record."[78] The *Los Angeles Times* put a delirious spin on Webster's commission appointment, stating that "he demonstrated skill in rooting out misconduct," and that he "exudes a charming manner and has honed a highly competitive tennis game—qualities that make him a popular Washington insider." Webster left the CIA and joined the Washington law office of Milbank, Tweed, Hadley & McCloy in September 1991. John McCloy, a deceased senior partner, was avidly pro-Nazi, having freed a number of ranking Nazis at Nuremburg. McCloy also sat on the Warren Commission, vigorously scuttling any evidence that might incriminate the CIA and Pentagon in John Kennedy's murder.[79] One of Webster's colleagues at the law firm is Thomas Pucchio, who "investigated" E.F. Hutton and Merrill Lynch in the 1980s, and managed to overlook the washing of heroin profits through Swiss banks. Elliot Richardson of the Iran-contra affair is also employed by the firm.[80] "It was Elliot Richardson," wrote Robert Kephart, the publisher of *Human Events*, "who very actively promoted the initial federal grant for psychosurgical experimentation." Kephart commented that he thought this would be of interest to anyone concerned with "the onrushing Orwellian state."

Top: Elliot Richardson—Bottom: Richard Stone, right, with Daniel Ortega of the Nicaraguan Junta

The third-ranking member of the Webster Commission, Richard Stone, comes from the legal offices of the Department of Defense.[81]

Recommendations were drawn up by representatives of the CIA, defense contractors, corporate attorneys and the military. Why? "Since the Watts ghetto uprising," writes former UCLA professor and political researcher Donald Freed, "domestic counter-insurgency has become a 'growth industry.' Forty thousand fast-growing police agencies, containing more than 400,000 men and women, are becoming chief customers for many defense industry contractors." With the murder of Martin Luther King and bloody outbursts in Detroit and Watts in the 1960s, "defense stocks soared. Giant conglomerates . . . now compete with vigor for the ballooning domestic defense budget." The disburser of these funds is the LEAA, the recipient of grant-in-aid money exceeding $1 billion a year. That billion dollars, according to a House subcommittee on monetary affairs, has purchased "inefficiency, waste, maladministration and, in some cases, corruption."[82]

This dismal formula translates to the defense firms represented by the Christopher and Webster Commissions, linked together by an obscure but powerful agency known as the Defense Industrial Security Command, or DISC. This ominous secret police organization is controlled by executives of the huge defense firms, DIA, CIA and the domestic intelligence division of the FBI. The Mafia also has a substantial interest in the operation of DISC through ownership of some defense-related corporations. (Treasury Secretary Lloyd Bentsen has long been graciously supported by DISC executives—to the tune of $7 million in 1970, channeled through a series of CIA covers—and was a leading force in the ruination of two Texas S&Ls.) DISC has secretly financed Congressmen who support legislation

Top: Timothy Goldman—Bottom, from right: John Mack, president of the Los Angeles Urban League; Derek Carr, manager of the burned-out market in the background; then-Sen. John Seymour (R-Calif.); then-President George Bush. The others are unidentified.

favoring defense spending. Ronald Reagan has also received generous covert campaign funding from this secret police organization. DISC has been directly tied to the assassinations of President Kennedy and Martin Luther King. Many members of the panels entrusted with investigating the L.A. riots have worked for DISC firms. Some assisted in the cover-up of Kennedy's murder and have Mafia ties.

The Orwellian penumbra of the intelligence establishment imposed itself again with the FBI's handling of photographic evidence. A freelance reporter seeking riot footage a few days after the beating of Reginald Denny, Gregory Sandoval, met retired Air Force Captain Timothy Goldman, who had videotaped the bludgeoning from the street. Before the tapes were confiscated by police and FBI for use in the Denny beating trial, Sandoval peddled them on the television news circuit. They aired on CNN, all three networks and KTLA. Sandoval took a cut of Goldman's substantial royalties, the initial payment being $20,000. Unlike George Holliday, who became something of a folk hero after videotaping the Rodney King incident, Goldman found himself besieged with death threats, he says, and was forced into hiding.[83] The LAPD has since appealed to the FCC to ban future helicopter television coverage of any violent mass civil disorder in the city.

The maelstrom of the L.A. riots was only a harbinger—behind the obscuring veil of the corporate press, covert operators move the country toward open fascism. Provocateurs tear at the center of society, and ersatz investigative commissions only tilt tax revenue away from starving social programs into the coffers of defense firms, paramilitarists and secret police, fattening themselves on the misery of L.A.'s minorities. All ultimately pay for ignoring their screams.

Epilogue:
Time Machine—Watts, 1965

The fires were set again, rage sterilized the city. When the smoke cleared, thirty-four families grieved. The war between the invisible government and L.A.'s minorities shifted to the courts and council chambers.

The coroner's inquest into riot homicides, overseen by Deputy Coroner Charles Langhauser, was denounced as a "whitewash" by one attorney. He was ejected from the proceedings. The jury (seven of the nine were white) listened to the testimony of officers regarding the homicide of Homer Ellis of East 33rd Street. Ellis, an accused looter, died of gunshot wounds to the chest. The police officers testified Ellis had been under the influence of alcohol. They were not cross-examined by dictate of the court.

Attorney Hugh Manes of the ACLU rose to his feet, demanded the right to cross-examine police witnesses. Langhauser restored order in the courtroom. Manes was thrown out. The jury deliberated for 40 minutes and ruled the killing a justifiable homicide.[84]

The same day, September 14th, 1965, Police Chief William Parker (the mentor of Daryl Gates) sparred with City Councilman Tom Bradley, a former police lieutenant, in a committee room. What exactly did Parker mean, Bradley mused, when he testified that an "organized effort" was made to escalate the Watts riot?

Parker mumbled something about a youth with a bullhorn. He said the police had identified the youth and linked him to an unnamed organization. Bradley asked if Parker could identify the youth and this organization.

"I'm not going to identify him," Parker retorted. "I'm not going to do anything on hearsay until I have legal evidence."

The day before, Chief Parker had testified in answer to questions

William Parker

regarding sundry patterns of coordination amid the violence. Encoded radio messages interrupting normal police channels were cited by Chief Parker as "further evidence of organization." Clandestine radio messages, of course, are the imprimatur of secret police agencies.[85]

Parker said that further evidence of planning and organization came after the riot when, on a Labor Day weekend, the police department was subjected to a widespread "psychological warfare campaign," indicating that new rioting was about to start.

Evidence that the chaos had been incited cropped up everywhere. At an address before the Portland American Legion, conservative Republican Sen. George Murphy of California laid blame on "vicious groups of trained troublemakers."[86] The L.A. Police, Fire and Civil Defense Committee reported there were "definite patterns," leading to the conclusion that there was some form of coordination. The committee said that rioting along 103rd Street in Watts "involved persons who are not generally considered residents of the area."[87] The McCone Commission found no proof of prior planning, but charged that "inflammatory hand-bills" were distributed before the riot broke out—"the work of several gangs whose membership of young men range in age from 14 to 35 years."[88]

Mayor Sam Yorty wasn't mincing words. He blamed communist agitation. Yorty told a Congressional committee that "known communists" had waged "a worldwide campaign to stigmatize all police as brutal. The cry of police brutality has been shouted in cities all over the world by communists, dupes and demagogues irrespective of the facts." J. Edgar Hoover agreed, claiming that "for years it has been communist policy to charge 'police brutality' in a calculated campaign to discredit law

Sam Yorty

enforcement and to accentuate racial issues. The riots and disorders of the past three years clearly highlight the success of this communist smear campaign."[89]

However prevalent the communist agitation, police and soldiery were hamstrung in August 1965 by the negligence of law enforcement officials, as they would be in 1992. The California National Guard was called out six hours after Chief Parker requested assistance. The official order was signed by the lieutenant governor at 5:15 p.m. The telephone call to the governor's office was placed at 11:00 a.m., when the melee on the streets was out of control. By mid-afternoon, Chief Parker grumbled that he'd asked for Guard troops and could not understand the delay. Lt. Gov. Glenn Anderson, who eventually signed the order, received the emergency call from Parker in the absence of Gov. Pat Brown, and left to attend a meeting at the University of California board of regents. In the meantime, the incineration of the ghetto was spreading.[90]

As for police, Chief Parker explained on the day following the first outburst that they stayed outside the original site of rioting, "so that we wouldn't be an irritant."[91]

The whitewash was slightly soiled around the edges. After the Watts riots, a powerful designate of the Washington security "elite" stepped forward to martinize any evidence of provocation. John McCone was CIA director when John Kennedy was murdered. He first testified at a Warren Commission hearing that Lee Harvey Oswald's connections to the Agency were "minor," when everyone around Oswald was in fact a CIA mover or flunky. Contradictory testimony at his next appearance was straightened by Counterintelligence Chief James Angleton, who rehearsed the leading CIA witnesses with note cards. "REPLIES THAT WILL BE GIVEN" at

John McCone

the hearing, Angleton directed, would include:

Q: Was Oswald an agent of the CIA?
A: No.
Q: Does the CIA have any evidence showing that a conspiracy existed to assassinate President Kennedy?
A: No.[92]

McCone, like Angleton, was a Knight of Malta, the Vatican's centuries-old military order, allies of genocidal third-world dictators, Nazis, Mafia and the CIA.[93] The staunch ultra-conservative had amassed a great personal fortune in the steel and construction industries. McCone was appointed by John Kennedy to head the CIA as a concession to Republicans. The administration had come close to shutting down the Agency's mind control program, but it was McCone who convinced Robert Kennedy to continue funding for brain and behavior experimentation.[94] He was also "keen" on the idea of dropping a nuclear bomb on Cuba.[95] After Kennedy was assassinated, William Bishop, a military intelligence officer considered by some to be a central conspirator, was discovered to have in his possession a file of phone numbers, including those of ace CIA pilot David Ferrie and Director John McCone.[96]

The McCone Report pinpointed racial and economic discrimination as the underpinnings of urban unrest in L.A., as would the Christopher Commission's report nearly 30 years later. (Chief Parker had his own thoughts on the riot's causes, namely the erosion of respect for the law, and a constant flow of "propaganda" to the ghettos claiming that blacks are economically deprived.[97]) Unfortunately, as Warren Christopher admits, public officials totally ignored the social and political recommendations of the McCone panel.[98] The report however did become a touchstone for beefing up the red squads and secret police units.

The regression to para-fascistic police methods is only possible in a vacuum of accountability. Three decades following the turmoil of Watts, oversight is still almost nonexistent. From the Christopher report: "Although the City Charter assigned the Police Commission ultimate control over [Police] Department policies, its authority . . . is illusory." The commission is passive, "essentially acting as a 'booster' for the department." Councilman Zev Yaroslavsky, responding to the report, said, "The message is that without civilian oversight, the Police Department can run amok. . . . Every major problem that has risen in the Police Department was because of a lack of oversight."[99] As for L.A.'s minorities, caged birds rarely sing.

1965

1992

Source File

1. "Site of Denny Beating Wasn't Riot Flash Point, Gates Says," *Los Angeles Times*, May 13, 1992, p. A18.

2. *Ibid.*

3. "Officials See No Proof of Gang Plot to Ignite Riots," *Los Angeles Times*, July 25, 1992, p. B1.

4. "Caught Off-Guard: A Culver City guardsman was arrested during riots," *Santa Monica Evening Outlook*, May 6, 1992, p. A3.

5. "Mistrial declared in riot-related Beverly Hills case," *Santa Monica Evening Outlook*, September 19, 1992, p. A3.

6. "Arrested the First Night, on Guard Duty Next Day," *Los Angeles Times*, May 6, 1992, p. A11.

7. *Santa Monica Evening Outlook*, May 6, 1992.

8. "Ex-Convict 'Recruited' for Rioting," *San Francisco Chronicle*, July 26, 1973.

9. Citizens Research and Investigations Committee and Louis Tackwood, *The Glass House Tapes*, New York: Avon Press, 1973, p. 5.

10. *Ibid.*, pp. 213-214.

11. "Why is the Senate Watergate Committee Functioning as Part of the Cover-Up," *The Realist*, December 1972, p. 21.

12. *Ibid.*

13. Mike Rothmiller and Ivan G. Goldman, *L.A. Secret Police*, New York: Pocket Books, 1992, p. 9.

14. "Judge Slapped Gag Order on Trial of 7 Deputies," *Los Angeles Times*, October 24, 1990, p. B1.

15. "King Aftermath Rekindles Police Spying Controversy," *Los Angeles Times*, June 18, 1991, p. A1.

16. *Ibid.*

17. *Ibid.*

18. *Ibid.*

19. "Bomb Disarmed at Airport, Turkish Team Threatened," *Los Angeles Times*, August 14, 1984, p. A1.

20. "Officer Charged with Planting Bomb on Bus," *Los Angeles Times*, October 15, 1984, p. A1.

21. "Ex-Officer Gets Probation for Olympic Bomb Ruse," *Los Angeles Times*, October 5, 1985, p. B1.

22. *The Glass House Tapes*, pp. 41-42.

23. Frank Donner, "The Confessions of an FBI Informer," *Harper's*, December 1972, p. 54. Also, "Gainesville," *Counterspy*, Fall 1973, pp. 22-25: The trial of the

Gainesville Eight was "part of the Watergate cover-up."

24. "The Kent State Shootings," KPFK-FM, Los Angeles, May 3, 1989.

25. *Ibid.*

26. "Webster to Head Probe of Police Response to Riot," *Los Angeles Times*, May 12, 1992, p. A1.

27. Brussell, p. 21.

28. Interviews with residents.

29. "3 Suspects Seized in Beating of Truck Driver During Riot," *Los Angeles Times*, May 13, 1992, p. A1.

30. "New Mexico Asks Procunier for More Advice," *San Francisco Chronicle*, February 5, 1980. Also, "New Mexico Was Warned, Prison Was Primed for a Riot," *San Francisco Chronicle*, February 5, 1980.

31. *Los Angeles Times*, May 12, 1992.

32. *Ibid.*

33. "Lieutenant Sues Gates Over Criticism on Riot Response," *Los Angeles Times*, October 3, 1992, p. B1.

34. "Son's Overdose During Riots Preoccupied Him, Chief Says," *Los Angeles Times,* May 28, 1992, p. A7.

35. "Riot Found Police in Disarray—Officers Kept from Flash Point Despite Pleas," *Los Angeles Times*, May 6, 1992, p. A1.

36. "Police May Have Ignored Basic Riot Plan," *New York Times*, May 7, 1992, p. A22.

37. "Bush Sends Troops to L.A.," *Los Angeles Times*, May 3, 1992, p. A1.

38. "Riot Report Says Guard Bungled," *Los Angeles Times*, December 3, 1992, p. A1.

39. *Los Angeles Times*, May 12, 1992.

40. "Guard Takes Position After Delays, Snafus," *Los Angeles Times*, May 2, 1992, p. A1.

41. Peter J. Boyer, "Looking for Justice in L.A.," *The New Yorker* , March 15, 1993, p. 68.

42. *Ibid.*

43. Mike Davis, "L.A.: The Fire This Time," *Covert Action Information Bulletin*, Spring 1992, p. 13.

44. *Ibid.*, p. 16.

45. *Ibid.*, p. 20.

46. *Ibid.*, p. 18.

47. *Los Angeles Times*, May 13, 1993.

48. *Ibid.*, p. 20.

49. *Ibid.*

50. "Jury Dominated by Whites in L.A. Police Case," *The Independent* (U.K.),

February 24, 1993, p. 10. Eight jurors had served in the military, "prompting suspicions that this helped explain their pro-police sentiment."

51. "Riot Case Defense Corrupt?" *Santa Monica Evening Outlook*, October 2, 1992, p. A1.

52. "Attorney Tells of Discord in Denny Case Defense," *Los Angeles Times*, November 20, 1992, p. B2.

53. *Santa Monica Evening Outlook*, October 24, 1992. Also, "Hearing Ordered on Sabotage Allegations," *Los Angeles Times*, October 24, 1992, p. B3: In statements recorded by Celani, he contended, "the Center was created by federal law enforcement authorities and used to subvert the due process rights of accused criminals in this case and others."

54. "Lawyer Adds Bizarre Note to Denny Case," *Los Angeles Times*, August 13, 1992, p. B3.

55. Fredrick George Celani, *Affidavit in Support of a Petition for Writ of Habeas Corpus*, filed with the U.S. District Court for the state of California, January 1991. Celani writes that in return for collecting information inside the prison system, he would be granted parole "after one-third service of the term expired (July 1990)." The promise was not kept, he lamented, thus the motion for habeas corpus demanding his release from prison.

56. Philip Agee, *Inside the Company: A CIA Diary*, New York: Stone Hill, 1975, p. 611.

57. Boyer, p. 74.

58. *Ibid.*

59. *Los Angeles Times*, November 20, 1992.

60. *Santa Monica Evening Outlook*, October 24, 1992.

61. "Symbolism Alters Image of Suspects in Denny Beating" *Los Angeles Times*, December 27, 1992, p. A1. Rep. Maxine Waters (D-Los Angeles) said, "The case has not just been tainted. It's beyond just being tampered with."

62. Boyer, p. 78.

63. *Times* columnist Bob Sipchen reviews Boyer's March 15 *New Yorker* article on Celani in "the L.A. 4: Is Their Case Beyond Hope of Justice?" *Los Angeles Times*, March 3, 1993, p. B1.

64. It can be presumed that attorneys for Mannatt had some inkling of his clandestine activities, and those of his colleagues.

65. "Powerful Players Get Global Bank Off the Ground," *Washington Times*, April 24, 1988.

66. Mae Brussell, World Watchers International report, KAZU-FM, Monterey, California, May 23, 1988.

67. Foundation Center, *The Foundation Directory*, 10th Edition, New York, 1985, entry No. 676.

68. Obituary, *New York Times*, December 2, 1991, p. D10.

69. David France, *Bag of Toys: Sex, Scandal, the Death Mask Murder*, New York: Warner Books, 1992. Kasanov, according to France, was a player in the rigged murder trial. Crispo was acquitted of murder charges, but a plant in the jury managed to pull this off with a series of blatant manipulations of other jurors. The corruption in the judicial proceedings was obvious even to casual participants in the trial, as it must have been to Kasanov. The New York attorney was a director of the Legal Aid Society, but his clients were strictly corrupt high rollers. Kasanov's involvement in the non-profit legal organization recalls the allegations of Fred Celani regarding covert manipulations of criminal defense cases at his own legal center in Los Angeles.

70. *Ibid.* Entire account is given in *Bag of Toys*, pp. 315-341, statements on jury tampering, pp. 340-341.

71. "Marietta's Ex-Chief, Paisley Tied—Long Relationship Revealed in Probe," *Washington Post*, June 19, 1991, p. B1.

72. "Leaders of Riot Response Probe Have Top Credentials," *Los Angeles Times*, May 13, 1992, p. B1.

73. Personal correspondence—Diane Bauer, Children's Defense Fund, to Jeremy Stone, director of the Federation of American Scientists, December 20, 1973. "LEAA," wrote Bauer, "appears to be getting deeper into quasi-medical research." Dr. West's Center, she noted, "would apparently be the *eighth* such LEAA-backed project."

74. Ralph Miller, "Psycho-Surgery: Childhood's End," *Clear Creek*, June 1972, p. 20.

75. Peter Schrag, *Mind Control*, New York: Delta Books, 1978, pp. 1-5.

76. Brussell, *The Realist*, December 1972, p. 24. The LEAA also backed the castration of male prisoners and experiments in convulsive-shock therapy.

77. Davis, *Covert Action Information Bulletin*, p. 16.

78. David Corn, "BCCI Report? What BCCI Report?" *The Nation*, October 26, 1992, p. 460.

79. Kai Bird, *The Chairman: John J. McCloy, the Making of the American Establishment*, New York: Simon & Schuster, 1992, pp. 330-375 (on Nazis), also pp. 548-566 (on the Warren Commission).

80. "Former CIA Director Joins New York Law Firm," *Wall Street Journal*, September 26, 1991, p. B2.

81. *Los Angeles Times*, May 12, 1992. The notice on Stone appears on p. A18.

82. *The Glass House Tapes*, pp. 222-223.

83. Frank Donner, "Bearing Witness," *People* Magazine, January 25, 1993, p. 82.

84. "Death in Riot Ruled 'Justifiable Homicide'" *Los Angeles Times*, September 15, 1965, p. A3.

85. "Parker and Bradley Clash at Riot Inquiry," *Los Angeles Times*, September 15, 1965, p. A3.

86. "Troublemakers Caused Riots, Murphy Says," *Los Angeles Times*, August 25, 1965, p. A24.

87. "Many Causes of Riots Held Beyond City Help," *Los Angeles Times*, November 27, 1965, p. A16.

88. "Violence in the City—An End or a Beginning," *McCone Report*, December 2, 1965, pp. 22-23.

89. U.S. News & World Report, *Communism and the New Left*, Washington, D.C., 1970, pp. 85-86.

90. "Order to Guard Given 5 Hours After Request," *Los Angeles Times*, August 15, 1965, p. A1.

91. *Los Angeles Times*, September 15, 1965, p. A3.

92. Warren Hinckle and William Turner, *The Fish is Red: The Story of the Secret War Against Castro*, New York: Harper & Row, 1981, p. 228.

93. Jonathan Vankin, *Conspiracies, Cover-Ups and Crimes: From JFK to the CIA Terrorist Connection*, New York: Dell Books, 1992, p. 207.

94. Gordon Thomas, *Journey into Madness: The True Story of Secret CIA Mind Control and Medical Abuse*, New York: Bantam Books, 1989, p. 232.

95. Laton McCartney, *Friends in High Places: The Bechtel Story—The Most Secret Corporation and How it Engineered the World*, New York: Simon & Schuster, 1988, p. 111.

96. Dick Russell, *The Man Who Knew Too Much*, New York: Carroll & Graf, 1992, p. 420.

97. "Parker Warns Disrespect for Law Perils U.S.," *Los Angeles Times*, August 22, 1965, p. A1.

98. Robert Scheer, "Clinton's Globe-Trotter," *Los Angeles Times Magazine*, February 21, 1993, p. 18.

99. "Reaction to Report," *Los Angeles Times*, July 10, 1991, p. A15.

Photo Credits

P. 8: REED SAXON - AP / Wide World Photos
P. 10: DOUGLAS C. PIZAC - AP / Wide World Photos
P. 12: ROBERT CARL COHEN
P. 14: PAT McMILLAN
P. 16: PAUL SAKUMA - AP / Wide World Photos
P. 18: ROY HAYES
P. 20, top: MATHEW - AP / Wide World Photos
P. 20, bottom: LENNOX McLENDON - AP / Wide World Photos
P. 20, inset: BEN OLENDER - *Los Angeles Times*
P. 22, top: AP / Wide World Photos
P. 22, bottom: AP / Wide World Photos
P. 24: AP / Wide World Photos
P. 26: DOUGLAS C. PIZAC - AP / Wide World Photos
P. 28: AP / Wide World Photos
P. 30, top: MICHAEL TWEED - AP / Wide World Photos
P. 30, bottom: JULIE MARKS - AP / Wide World Photos
P. 32: PAUL SAKUMA - AP / Wide World Photos
P. 34: Official U.S. Army photograph
P. 36: BABETO MATTHEWS - AP / Wide World Photos
P. 38: Denny family album - AP / Wide World Photos
P. 40: KEVORK DJANSEZIAN - AP / Wide World Photos
P. 42: NICK UT - AP / Wide World Photos
P. 44: *The State Journal-Register*
P. 48: MARSHA T. GORMAN - *Los Angeles Times*
P. 50: *The State Journal-Register*
P. 52: JOHN DURICKA - AP / Wide World Photos
P. 54, top: AP / Wide World Photos
P. 54, bottom: BARRY SWEET - AP / Wide World Photos
P. 56: AP / Wide World Photos
P. 58: CHRIS MARTINEZ - AP / Wide World Photos
P. 60, top: AP / Wide World Photos
P. 60, bottom: JUAN MALTES - AP / Wide World Photos
P. 62, top: NICK UT - AP / Wide World Photos
P. 62, bottom: MARCY NIGHSWANDER - AP / Wide World Photos
P. 64: AP / Wide World Photos
P. 66: AP / Wide World Photos
P. 68: AP / Wide World Photos
P. 70: AP / Wide World Photos
P. 72: AP / Wide World Photos
P. 73 and Inside Covers: AP / Wide World Photos
P. 74: CRAIG FUJII - AP / Wide World Photos
P. 79: KCAL TV via CNN - AP / Wide World Photos
Outside Covers: Color photo credits are listed on p. 4